CONTENTS

INTRODUCTION

Kissing is the single most important means of communication today, and yet very little time or effort is spent analysing its technique and effectiveness. In most cases the emphasis is placed on quantity rather than quality. At parties discoteques and such like gatherings, kisses are dished out like hot water at a 'Kettle makers convention'. Come to think of it, most of them are not too dissimilar to hot water; they are wet, warm and pretty tasteless.

This book will attempt to explore the intricacies of the art of kissing, and present answers to the question: "Why are some kisses like fighting with a wet sponge, whilst others make the knees go weak?"

The course must be studied carefully, and enough time allocated to practising the techniques, preferably on someone else. For those of your who are pretty hopeless, we suggest you begin by practising on household objects rather than people.

Whatever   stage you may be at, we are confident that by the end of this book, your kisses too, will be like fireworks. Even if they are not, the diploma in kissing -which you will get at the end of this course- may help you to pretend that they are and equip you to con your way through those tricky situations.

1 - WHAT IS A KISS?

Before we explore the mysteries of the kissing act, and all that goes with it, it is a good idea to try and understand the basics.

Kissing possesses a language of its own. There are many kinds of kisses, each with its own meaning and intention. Confusing the different catergories can be disastrous and may lead to a missed opportunity. A pocket size dictionary at hand may prove invaluable.

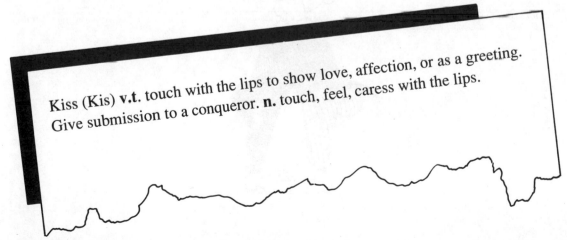

Kiss (Kis) **v.t.** touch with the lips to show love, affection, or as a greeting. Give submission to a conqueror. **n.** touch, feel, caress with the lips.

2 - THE FUNCTIONS OF A KISS

a) The Polite Kiss

A polite kiss, as the word indicates, is given because it would be impolite not to. There are several situations where one can speak of "Polite Kissing". Take a Western politician who goes East for a state visit. He steps off the plane, and straight into the arms of his host, no one knows whether they really do kiss, or just check each other's shoulder pads, they may even be biting each others' earlobe's whilst murmering a swearword. For the benefit of this book, we will assume that they are exchanging a 'polite kiss'.

"Polite Kisses" are also given when presents are exchanged. The presents themselves are irrelevant; they could be, and usually are, the most useless things one could imagine, like a tenth tie, or something you would not be seen dead wearing. The polite kiss in these situations is guaranteed, and is usually accompanied by the phrase "Thank you, it's just what I wanted".

Polite Kisses are usually given out of respect and not for pleasure. Unless you fancy the person that you respect.

b) The Greeting Kiss

It is a matter of opinion, whether the political kiss discussed earlier, could also, count as a 'Greeting Kiss'. Even individuals who hate each other's guts, indulge in the exchange of the 'Greeting Kiss'.

Greeting Kisses have become quite fashionable in today's society. A few years ago, the unknown and vague acquaintances were usually greeted with a mere hand shake, and kisses were reserved for close friends and family.
Today, this distinction is rapidly disappearing.

Greeting Kisses are no more than the smacking of the lips brushing the cheeks. They vanish in the air, but leave all sorts of smells and colours on your cheeks.
It is comforting to know that you can exchange these kisses, without having to take your hands out of your pockets.

c) Affectionate Kiss

The affectionate and loving kisses are given to show one's love for that individual. A budding love could start with an affectionate kiss.

Affectionate kisses are seldom placed on the cheeks. If they are, it is usually a part of a bigger 'ritual'. The mouth is the favourite closely followed by the ear, neck and hands.

d) The Kiss of Love

The 'Kiss of love' is usually given with the eyes rather than the lips, and it is almost always the start of more to come. Many have ended up in high grass after such a kiss. We will not go into details just yet.

It is worth pointing out that despite the extensive research into the complexities of a kiss, there are still those who are of the opinion that kissing is such a natural thing, there is no need to learn it. This may be the case in theory, but in practice, many have fallen flat on their faces; going for the kill without ammunition.

The younger people are amongst those most vulnerable to doubt and lack of self confidence, particularly during the first years of kissing. Sometimes they worry that perhaps they are not doing it well enough, or even, what if the other person is doing it better. There are even those who believe that one could actually get pregnant just by kissing. This is of course quite possible, provided the kiss is right.

INVESTIGATION

Serious investigations have taken place to establish the origin of the "kiss of love". Unfortunately the researchers were unable to reach an agreement, but some rather interesting theories resulted. One of the theories is that the "love kiss" originates from the sucking reflexes of a baby.

Others are of the opinion that the kiss derived from a certain kind of 'love biting', which some animals still partake in.

The fact of the matter is that a "love kiss" is often a mixture of kisses and minute bites, or nibbling if you like.

3 - THE EFFECT OF SMELLS AND SOUNDS ON KISSING

Smells

Human beings are categorised into three groups according to their scents.
a) People whose smell is of a pleasant nature; be it natural or through artificial means; perfumes etc..
b) People who do not have a noticeable smell; good or bad.
c) The skunks.

With animals, smells play a very important role. Sexual excitement in some animals produces smells, irresistible to their opposite sex. Neutralising these smells would almost wipe out the dumb animal's sex life.

Human beings react less to smells; though there are those who sometimes wish that they could blame their pathetic sex life on their neutralised love smells. It is in fact their overactive sweat glands triggered by their kiss passions, but sadly for them, they are positioned in the wrong parts of the body such as the feet, etc..

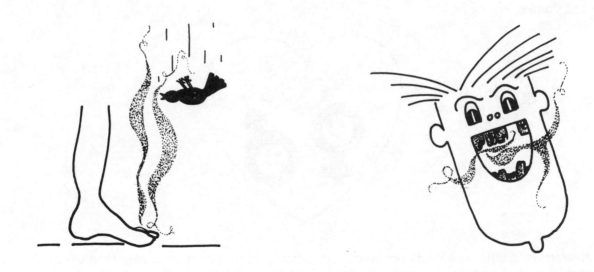

Another source of smell is the mouth. In some people this smell is mild enough to be neutralised by the other peson's natural mouth smells. Others less fortunate, however, are those who can offer a long lasting general anaesthetic, just by opening their mouths.

If you are amongst those whose bad breath is merely a result of daily habits such as smoking, drinking or even visiting the local curry house; then, please keep a gas mask handy for your partner, and avoid having to make those unnecessary sacrifices.

Sounds

Those who indulge in the very passionate kiss, may have experienced those unconscious mating sounds while kissing. These usually take the form of whispered sweet nothings or merely groans and moans. These sounds are normal, and usually help to intensify the passion, if done correctly.

4 - KISSING, WHAT DO YOU NEED?

Basically all you need to indulge in the "kissing act" is your mouth. It would of course help if there was someone else with you; but this for some people is not necessary, as they are content with their own bodies; their arms, hands and legs etc., and for hard to reach places, they use a mirror.

Kissing on one's own is one thing, doing it with someone else can be a more pleasurable experience. Finding the right person to kiss however can be a very painstaking experience requiring persistence.

There are of course guidelines, set by society, as to who can kiss who. It is fine for a man to kiss a woman, a woman to kiss a woman, but not for a man to kiss a man. So two brothers greeting each other after many years of being apart must restrict their emotions to a mere hand shake.

PUZZLE

For those of you with no one to kiss, here is a puzzle to cheer you up. Find as many of the hidden words relating to kissing as you can, by going up down or diagonally.

P	O	E	D	A	F	I	M	A	D	O	smacker
A	E	D	C	F	C	O	O	B	E	C	peck
U	W	C	M	O	C	L	U	D	A	K	tongue
A	T	T	K	N	H	C	T	F	R	C	kiss
T	O	N	G	U	E	E	H	L	E	U	mouth
C	T	O	P	H	E	O	K	I	S	S	lips
K	O	S	S	I	K	L	L	P	T	E	dearest
S	M	A	C	K	E	R	O	S	M	N	suck

The answer can be found of page 59.

23

5 - MOUTHS

The shape, form and size of an individual's mouth reveals more about their character than any other part of his or her anatomy.
You can tell whether a person is kind, miserable, passionate, or even a compulsive nagger just be looking at their mouth.

MOUTH 1... ANALYSIS

CHARACTER
People with this type of mouth look at life optimistically, but are by no means gullible. They are partygoers and enjoy most kinds of music.

OCCUPATION
Not suitable for jobs that require leadership, unless acquired by mistake, in which case they are absolute failures.

FOOD
They are compulsive eaters, eating anything that's put in front of them. As a result they are usually over weight.

CLOTHES
Fashion conscious, brand conscious; with a weak spot for big baggy bright coloured clothes.

HOLIDAYS
Beach and sea, topless. They love staying out all night.

KISSING
They enjoy kissing, and never stop.

MOUTH 2... ANALYSIS

CHARACTER
A sourlooking, pinched little mouth which also sums up this type of person's character. With them, nothing is ever just right. Everything is either too dry or too wet, too sweet or too salty, too hot or too cold. People with this type of mouth have had too little love, pocket money and attention throughout their life.

OCCUPATION
They like to think that they are born leaders, and usually are in places such as a vinegar and pickle factory, a sewing room, a toilet seat testing room, etc..

FOOD
They are fussy, picky eaters who eat the same foods over and over again.

CLOTHES
Their clothes sense is usually about twenty years out of date. They never throw anything away, nor buy anything new.

HOLIDAY
Long walking expeditions. Cheap bed and breakfasts. They never venture out to the beach or the seaside, if they do, it is whilst fully clothed.

KISSING
Kissing, to them, is unhygenic

MOUTH 3... ANALYSIS

CHARACTER
They are always bemused by things happening around and to them. They often do as they are told, and hardly ever use their initiative.

OCCUPATION
Subservient. "Let someone else tell me what to do, then there is no chance of it going wrong".

FOOD
As far as food is concerned, they are not too fussy, but have to be forced to try something new.

CLOTHES
Not consipcuous. Moderately fashion conscious. Sober colours.

HOLIDAY
They are open to suggestions as long as everything is prearranged for them.

KISSING
They only kiss when they are kissed, and hardly ever take the initiative.

MOUTH 4...ANALYSIS

CHARACTER
They are very critical, moan quite a lot, but always keep cheerful, and never stop laughing. They are constantly finding faults with themselves, but never decide to put things right.

OCCUPATION
Their subordinates never seem to do anything right, while at the same time their boss doesn't appreciate them.

FOOD
They eat a lot of very fatty foods, drink like a fish, and frequently attempt to give up smoking.

CLOTHES
Proper and unnoticeable. They wear suits with sober ties and shining shoes.

HOLIDAYS
They usually have more important things to do.

KISSING
They only kiss on the cheek, and that is only if they are forced to.

MOUTH 5... ANALYSIS

CHARACTER
Neither here nor there. Crying and laughing are too closely linked for these people. A little tedious, but they can be unexpectedly witty at a party. They have a quiet expectant attitude to life, and change their underwear everyday, as they say, "You never know what might happen".

OCCUPATION
No managerial capabilities. Fiddlers, therefore very suitable for research work, computerwork, etc..

FOOD
Eat plain food, but like to go over board at times. They are not fussy about what they drink, as long as they drink.

CLOTHES
Well dressed especially whilst at work. They buy new clothes now and then, but only if it is sold to them half price.

HOLIDAY
They like quiet, well organised holidays spent in one place.

KISSING
They are shy to start with, but once they get going, there is no stopping them.

MOUTH 6... ANALYSIS

CHARACTER
Kind hearted people who can be pretty sharp and a little too confident at times. They are reliable happy people with perfect teeth. Their lips are what you might call made for kissing.

OCCUPATION
They are excellent at jobs which require good representation and lots of contact.

FOOD
They eat a lot, and relish their food. They are usually chubby, and constantly try new diets without any success.

CLOTHES
Colourful trousers, skirts, and saucy underwear.

HOLIDAYS
Beach, sun and sea in hot climates. Dance the night away, eat, sleep and back to the beach is their favourite routine.

KISSING
Often and with pleasure, though sometimes a little too wet.

6 - THE MECHANICS OF THE MOUTH

The mouth is made up of three main elements; the lips, the tongue, and the teeth. Each in turn playing a role and contributing to the pleasures of kissing.

The lips, being the most sensitive of the three, assess the potential kisser with the first touch, and then with the help of the eyes make the necessary signals of approval for more.

The tongue, being the most important of the three, uses its comprehensive network of tastebuds to taste and send messages to the brain on a number of intruders; from food, drink to foreign tongues.

Each section of the tongue has its own specific function and sensitivity, and performs accordingly.

1 - Temperature; heat, coolness etc.
2 - Flavour; sweetness, bitterness etc.
3 - Memory of the tastes already experienced
4 - Character; the love, hate, deceit etc. of the kisser.

So those of you who make a habit of being unfaithfull or deceitful, better watch out, your kiss might give the game away.

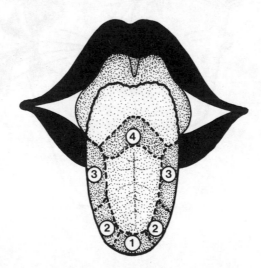

The teeth also play an important role in the act of kissing. If you find that hard to believe, just imagine kissing someone without them! The teeth are used to show one of two basic feelings:

a) Uncertainty and doubt; in which case the teeth are used to block the other person's advance, until such time as more information about that person is acquired.

b) Passion and true love. Here the teeth are used to inflict subtle bites on the other person's lips, tongue etc. etc.

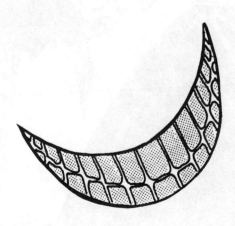

Kiss on the hand

7 - THE VARIOUS TYPES OF KISSES

We will asume that by now you have a sufficient knowledge to go straight to the actual kissing. Here, we introduce you to the various types of kisses that exist.

FOOTKISS
This type of kiss is reserved for people you respect and have high admiration for, for example the Pope, your mother in law etc.

KISS ON THE HAND
This one is given in very civilised circles. The man usually kisses the lady's hand, however that is not always the case. It originates from the time when bold patches indicated experience and wisdom. The ladies in those days would only kiss a man on the lips if he proved to be one such person. So the men bent down to show their bold patch, while at the same time kissing the lady's hand to reveal the reason why they were showing their bold patch.

THE DISTANT KISS
These kisses have been known to taste a lot nicer than some of the close up ones. They are exchanged at a distance where words cannot be used, and the gestures are meant to communicate hellos, goodbyes, etc. etc..

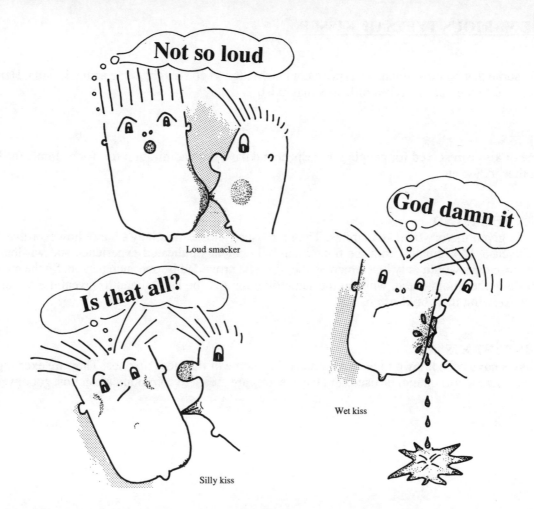

Loud smacker

Silly kiss

Wet kiss

36

NOISY KISS

This type of kiss is the speciality of those who kiss for the sake of kissing. Their kisses lack so many of the ingredients necessary for a good kiss, that they feel they have to make up for it with the exaggerated noise. Those under the influence of alcohol usually partake in this type of kiss; because the sense of hearing is normally the last thing to go when one gets drunk. Hearing it is the only way of knowing that a kiss is actually being exchanged.

WET KISS

A wet kiss is very similar to a noisy kiss, but worse. A wet kiss is normally given by people who have gone through an unhappy childhood, and some of their childhood habits; in this case 'dribbling', have been carried into their adult years.

KISS ON THE CHEEK

A kiss given on the cheek without any actual contact of the lips. The lips usually go through the motions, but end up kissing the air. This type of kiss is for those who would rather not kiss at all, but feel they have to make an effort.

SMACKER

A combination of the wet kiss and the noisy kiss; usually given to leave an impression, which they certainly do.

HUG

Not just a kiss, but also an embrace at the same time (shoulders, neck, hips or even bottoms). The kissing part of this is given on the cheek or the mouth, with the mouth firmly closed.

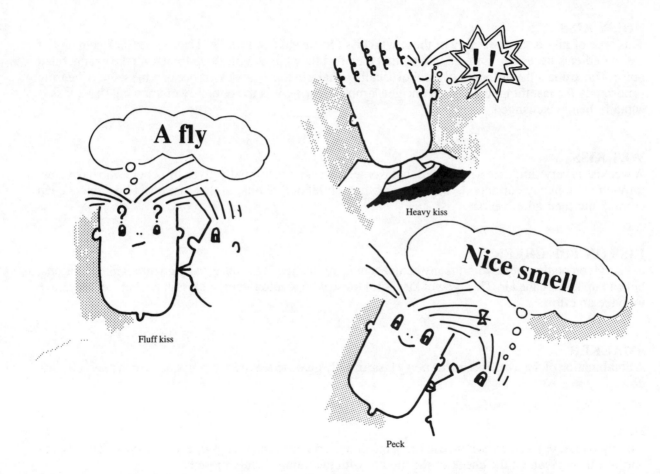

A fly

Fluff kiss

Heavy kiss

Nice smell

Peck

FRENCH KISS

At last, a real kiss.

Action: Press your lips firmly against your partner's, while at the same time keeping your mouth a little open. Suck in, and with luck, his/her tongue will appear in your mouth. Of course, you should not breath in each other's air, or else you may suffocate.

HEAVY KISS

A French kiss lasting a minimum of five minites. A knowledge of the basic breathing techniques are essential when participating in this type of kiss.

You should by now have experimented a number of different types of kisses; polite, greeting, liking, loving etc, and you should no longer be empty handed, or 'empty mouthed', as the case may be. Any how, good luck.

8 - PROBLEMS DURING KISSING

However talented you may be at kissing, there will always be those inevitable problems that will show their ugly faces when you least expect them. We will outline a few such problems, with possible solutions for each.

GLASSES
Glassess can be the most annoying obstacle when kissing, particularly when both parties are wearing them at the same time. The sound of clashing glasses is not the most romatic sounds; but one with possible solutions. Despite its disadvantages, contact lenses, can provide an easy solution. Alternatively, of course one could take the glasses off, as long as you are sure that the person in your arms is the person you wish to kiss. It is advisable not to keep the glasses in your shirt pocket when kissing, as you never know how passionate the kiss may turn out to be. Short-sighted people should strengthen their sense of smell, to avoid embarrassing encounters with the wrong people.

DIFFERING HEIGHTS

It is an accepted norm, that the woman should be slightly shorter than the man, so as to create a harmonious couple. She can then lay her little head on the man's broad chest, raise her yearning lips, and beg to be kissed.

This is of course not usually the case. There are couples who actually fall in love sitting down, and by the time they stand up, the dreaded cupid has already done its work. This is by no means a problem to be laughed at; some people consider this such a serious problem that they actually consider surgery. For others there are less painful solutions, though not quite as effective. One could of course try to go through life sitting down, or even lying down, but sooner or later, it becomes essential for the couple to stand on their feet. In these circumstances, one could perhaps try the simpler solutions readily available. The use of high heels, stairs, fences or even the clever use of pavement/street relationship, whereby the taller partner walks along the street, while the shorter walks along the edge of the pavement.

BAD BREATH

Bad breath is probably the most serious of all the problems, and one in which a considerable amount of tact and subtlety is needed by the suffering partner. Bombarding your partner with not so subtle little gifts such as toothpaste, toothbrushes, or even mouth spray, is not a good idea; unless of course they are personalised or even gold plated. Alternatively you could tell them about the special discounts your dentist is offering on bulk bookings. Whatever course of action you decide to take, and however hurtful it may turn out to be, remember it is better than a life time of holding you breath while kissing.

CLATTERING TEETH

Clattering, or losse fitting teeth can also have a paralising effect on love. In its worst case, you'll end up with your partner's teeth left in your mouth. A visit to the dentist or even some strong glue could easily solve the problem.

COSMETICS

There is nothing more annoying than kissing someone with lots of make up, and ending up with most of it on your face before the night is out. The waterproof/kissproof make up, available on the market, may lessen the problem, or alternatively, one could drop a subtle hint; like wearing a face mask just before kissing.

For those of you who are still not sure whether you are proficient enough to try the kiss on someone special, we have summarised all you need to know in four easy to follow steps.

STEP 1
You should never start with the lips, but rather work your way up to it by kissing the cheeks, the forehead, the neck and the ear. Do take your time, and use your lips imaginatively, and make sure the patch of skin being kissed is sucked though not enough to leave unsightly marks.

STEP 2
If all goes well with step 1, then its time to move closer to the lips, and only going for the lips themselves, if you are absolutely sure that the timing is right. Some people, particularly if they have just met, prefer to kiss with their mouths firmly shut. This is of course quite acceptable, providing it does not take too long before you try the more adventurous types of kisses.

STEP 3
The kiss on the lips should be carried out slowly and softly. Open your lips slightly, and by breathing in through your mouth, encourage your partner to move in with the tongue. Use the top of your tongues to explore each others; mouth, teeth, lips, the roof and all other sensitive parts.

STEP 4

You can now open your mouths a little wider, forming one mouth out of two. The saliva will begin to flow copiously, helping you become completely unaware of your surroundings. You will no longer hear the music, and the film may as well stop for all you care.

How you hold on to your partner whilst kissing is also important, and it should perhaps fall into one of the following three categories:

1- Your left arm over the right shoulder, and your right arm over the left hip of your partner. For the left-handed people, this position may be a little difficult at first.

2- Both arms around your partner's neck. A very comfortable position if your partner happens to be shorter than yourself.

3- Your arms around your partner's back, hips or bottom.

There are of course those who prefer to keep their hands in their pockets whilst kissing. Our experience has shown that these people are not to be trusted under any circumstances, particularly if they are amongst those who brag a lot.

9 - THE FIRST CONTACT

Making the first move is always the most dangerous part of any relationship. Apart from a shattered ego, one could also, depending on how violent your prey may turn out to be, experience physical pain. There are of course safe guards you can take before making a complete ass of yourself. You could perhaps try padding certain sensitive parts of your body, or even tying up your prey before trying anything on.

Alternatively, you could opt for the simpler form of detecting approval through the use of 'body language'.

You can be sure that a person is interested if he/she:

a) makes a fuss when you are around, and never stops calling you when you are not; usually with very silly excuses for calling you.

b) Continually stares at you. Here, it is worth checking that she/he is not one of those short sighted people who prefer not to wear glasses when socialising.

c) Is always trying to drag you in conversations by saying; "Don't you agree?" or "What do you think about this?".

d) 'Accidentally' keeps on touching you, usually the arms, knees etc.

e) Is terribly helpful (lets the air out of your tyres in order to help you pump it up), and in the process gain bonus points with you.

f) Blushes when in your company; chatting to them, or even just looking at them. This could of course be a sign of hate or anger.

g) Continually sends you perfumed notes etc.

h) Continually asks you to dance.

i) Continually seeks your company.

j) Makes a habit of forgetting his/her umbrella, in order to share yours.

OR

k) Is very straight forward, approaches you and tells you that he/she wants you.

Body language is usually sensed before it is seen, and once it is directed at you, you cannot miss it.

Tips on how to make yourself more approachable for the first contact:

a) Take a shower, wear clean clothes and eliminate any unpleasant body odours.

b) Brush your teeth, comb your hair, shave and make sure your zip is not undone.

c) Wear clothes that are comfortable and make you feel good. Particularly important if you are shy, being well dressed gives you the sense of security you need. Also make sure that what you are wearing is right for the occasion.

d) Use make up that does not run, and a hair style that stays put.

e) Don't talk about heavy topics; the other person may be just as thick as you.

f) Try to promote your good points. If you haven't any, then just lie lie lie.

10 - FACIAL EXPRESSIONS

The expression on peoples' faces is usually a good indication of exactly what they are thinking.
These expressions often fall into one of the following six categories:

1) **Quite fancies you**

OR he/she

- Has just been offered a drink by someone special.
- Has suddenly noticed the person who owes him/her some money.
- Is sitting on a very uncomfortable chair, but is afraid to move.
- Is thinking, oh no not him/her again. I must stop pretending to be interested.
- Has heard a joke ten times, but is trying to look amused.

2) Has not noticed you

OR he/she

- Is just fed up about life in general.
- Feels a little depressed.
- Has just been abandoned by his/her loved one.
- Has just had something stolen from him/her.
- Is thinking whether to complain about the stale crisps or the flat beer.
- Is feeling a little disappointed that no one has noticed him/her.

3) Does not want you (sorry)

OR he/she

- Is pretending not to know you.
- Is thinking, 'I wonder if I am sitting on something'.
- Is thinking whether he/she is talking to, is always this boring.
- Has split his/her trousers, and does not know how to make an exit.
- Is thinking, 'What have I done to deserve these weird friends?'
- Is wondering whether life in general is always as boring as this.

4) Has seen you before in his/her nightmares

OR he/she

- Has just seen someone who reminds him/her of their mother in law.
- Can't pay the bill, but is afraid to admit it.
- Has seen a mouse, but is determined to stay put.
- Has just realised that the curry they ordered was not one of the mild ones.
- Is thinking, 'What if he/she starts talking to me'.
- Is thinking, 'I wonder if anyone has noticed my new hair style?'
- "FIRE"

5) TAKE A HIKE

OR he/she

- Has a terrible headache, possibly caused by you.
- Just wants to pick on someone, but is too much of a coward.
- Is thinking, 'the next person to step on my foot is going to get it'.
- Is thinking, 'damn, my shoulder pads are on the move again'.
- Is just chewing on some very tough peanuts.
- Has just failed his/her driving test.

6) SORROW

OR he/she

- Wants to be comforted by you.
- Has seen you kissing someone else.
- Wants to go home to mummy.
- Has broken his/her zip, and has just been asked to dance by someone special.
- Is just dead drunk.

PUZZLE 1

Heart and Mouth
The first person who manages to place 3 mouths and 3 hearts in a row is the winner.

PUZZLE 2

Place the first letter of the following clues, to find the missing word.

1- You use it whilst French Kissing.
2- Always comes after the tenth kiss.
3- It is like kissing this, if your partner happens to be a smoker.
4- A greeting kiss is usually placed on this.
5- Some people kiss whilst wearing one on their head.
6- Four, two and five kisses add up to.
7- A provocative coloured lipstick.

11 - HOW TO LOOK APPROACHABLE

If you feel that perhaps you are not kissing as often as you wish, or are not even coming close to being approached; then it is just possible that you are not presenting the right image, or putting across the message in an effective way.

Cut out the 'KISS ME' stickers (on page 59), and pin them in a prominent position, and note the difference.

The way from heart to mouth.

You will find many detours from the heart to the mouth.

Search for the right way!

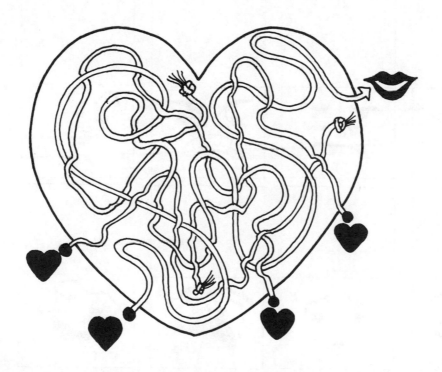

12 - HOW DO YOU FEEL?

To avoid misunderstandings, and to ensure a smooth 'Chat Up' phase, make sure that the other person knows exactly how you are feeling before going any further.

Cut out the correct image, and display it in your pocket etc.

SOLUTIONS TO THE PUZZLES

Puzzle on page 23

```
P  O  E  D  A  F  I   M  A   D  O
A  E  D  C  F  C  O   O  B   E  C
U  W  C  M  O  C  L   U  D   A  K
A  T  T  K  N  H  C   T  F   R  C
T  O  N  G  U  E  H   H  L  E  K  U
C  T  O  P  H  E  O   K  I  S   S
K  O  S  S  I  K  L   L  P  T   E
S  M  A  C  K  E  R   O  S  M   N
```

Stickers discussed on Page 56

Puzzle on page 55

The missing word:

T E A C H E R

13 - THE KISSING DIPLOMA

You should by now have mastered the art of kissing. If those around you have not yet noticed the difference; then cut out the diploma, fill it in and frame it. Hang it up in a prominent position, so that all your victims realise that how <u>you</u> kiss is how it should be done.

THE KISSING DIPLOMA

WE HEREBY CERTIFY THAT THE UNDERSIGNED

_____

HAS COMPLETED THE KISSING COURSE
TO THE SATISFACTION OF THE EXAMINERS

THE UNDERSIGNED MAY THEREFORE USE
THE TITLE:

DR. KISS

THE EXAMINER   THE TRAINEE

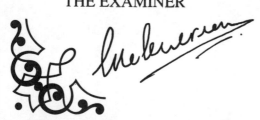

61

OTHER TITLES AVAILABLE FROM IDEAS UNLIMITED (PUBLISHING).

Please send me:

- ☐ copy/copies of **"100 Chat Up Lines"** ISBN 1-871964-00-8 (128 pages A7) — **@ £1.99** (postage free)
- ☐ copy/copies of **"Of course I Love You"** ISBN 1-871964-01-6 (96 pages A6) — **@ £1.99** (postage free)
- ☐ copy/copies of **"The Beginners Guide to Kissing"** ISBN 1-871964-02-4 (64 pages A5) — **@ £2.50** (postage free)
- ☐ copy/copies of **"Tips for a Successful Marriage"** ISBN 1-871964-03-2 (64 pages A5) — **@ £2.50** (postage free)
- ☐ copy/copies of **"The Joy of Fatherhood"** ISBN 1-871964-04-0 (64 pages A5) — **@ £2.50** (postage free)
- ☐ copy/copies of **"Office Hanky Panky"** ISBN 1-871964-05-9 (64 pages A5) — **@ £2.50** (postage free)

I Have enclosed a cheque/postal order for £............................. made payable to Ideas Unlimited (Publishing)

Name: ....

Address: ....

Fill in the coupon and send it with your payment to: **Ideas Unlimited (Publishing) PO Box 125, Portsmouth PO1 4PP**